How High Can an elephant Jump?

Written by Guy Campbell
Illustrated by Paul Moran

BARRON'S

First edition for the United States, its territories and possessions, Canada,
and the Phillippines published in 2008 by Barron's Educational Series, Inc.

First published in Great Britain in 2007 by Buster Books,
an imprint of Michael O'Mara Books Limited,
9 Lion Yard, Tremadoc Road, London SW4, 7NQ

Original edition copyright © 2007 by Buster Books
under the title *Do Elephants Ever Forget?*

All illustrations by Paul Moran.

All inquiries should be addressed to:
Barron's Educational Series, Inc.
250 Wireless Boulevard
Hauppauge, New York 11788
www.barronseduc.com

Library of Congress Control Number: 2008926686

ISBN-13: 978-0-7641-6171-1
ISBN-10: 0-7641-6171-7

Printed in Canada
9 8 7 6 5 4 3 2 1

Written by Guy Campbell
Illustrated by Paul Moran

CONTENTS

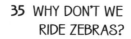

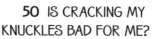

84 HOW MUCH ROOM IS THERE ON EARTH FOR EACH PERSON?

86 WHAT COLOR ARE A ZEBRA'S STRIPES?

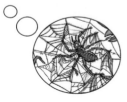

88 WHY DON'T SPIDERS STICK TO THEIR OWN WEBS?

90 WHY IS THE SKY BLUE?

92 COULD SCIENTISTS EVER BRING DINOSAURS BACK TO LIFE?

95 WHY AM I TIRED WHEN I HAVE JUST WOKEN UP?

98 HOW LONG COULD I LIVE ON NOTHING BUT COLA?

100 HOW HIGH CAN AN ELEPHANT JUMP?

102 HOW DOES MEDICINE MAKE ME FEEL BETTER?

105 IS THERE LIFE ON OTHER PLANETS?

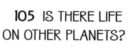

108 DO MEN OR WOMEN DRIVE BETTER?

110 WHAT'S THE WORST-SMELLING THING IN THE WORLD?

113 IF I COULD EAT ONLY ONE FOOD FOREVER, WHICH SHOULD I CHOOSE?

117 WHICH ANIMAL IS THE DEADLIEST IN THE WORLD?

119 WHAT MAKES SOMETHING FUNNY?

122 HOW DO FLIES WALK ACROSS A CEILING?

124 WHICH IS THE OLDEST ANIMAL IN THE WORLD?

INTRODUCTION

Have you ever wondered why yawns are so contagious? Or have you pondered why we don't ride zebras? And just how high *can* an elephant jump?

If you have ever puzzled over what would happen if a meteorite hit the earth, or the icecaps melted, look no further. If you have ever worried about sneezing with your eyes open, then this is the book for you.

How High Can An Elephant Jump? is a random and cool collection of fiendishly fascinating and perfectly perplexing questions and their answers. When everyone else is still scratching their heads, you'll have the answers right at your fingertips.

WILL MY EYEBALLS POP OUT IF I SNEEZE WITH MY EYES OPEN?

You may have heard scary stories warning that if you keep your eyelids open while sneezing, your eyeballs will fly out or your eardrums will burst. Is there any truth in these claims?

Sneezes are powerful bodily reactions and really shouldn't be messed with. When you sneeze, air is forced out of your nose or mouth at up to 102 miles (165 km) per hour. If you tried to stop a sneeze, by clamping your mouth shut and pinching your nose, you might force all that fast-moving air into your *eustachian* tubes (the passages that go from the back of your throat to the part of your ears called the middle ear). This could rupture your eardrums—causing acute pain and possibly, in extreme cases, deafness. Moreover, a sneeze carries germs, pollen, or dust (which your body is trying to get rid of by sneezing). This might get into your middle ear and cause infection.

When you sneeze, your eyes close automatically. This is called a *reflex action,* because you don't do it

consciously. The reason for this reflex action might be to keep your eyes from bulging uncomfortably during the sneeze. It might be to protect your eyes from possible infection from sneezed germs. Alternatively your eyes might shut because your facial muscles tense up in preparation for the upcoming explosion of air.

There are a few people who have managed to train themselves to keep their eyes open while sneezing, and their eyeballs don't pop out—honest. It is a difficult feat to perform, so you might ask, Why do they bother? Well, here's one reason why it might be useful: If you were driving a racing car at 70 miles (115 km) an hour, you could travel as far as 300 feet (90 m) while your eyes were shut during a sneeze! Pretty dangerous.

DO ELEPHANTS EVER FORGET?

To have a good memory you need to have a big brain and a lot of experiences. In that case, elephants certainly have the attributes needed to have an excellent memory.

Elephants have the largest brain of any land animal. An adult male African elephant's brain weighs about 10 pounds (5,000 g), which is massive if you compare it with an adult male human's brain, which weighs about 2.8 pounds (1,400 g), and a cat's brain, which weighs only around 1 ounce (30 g). As for experiences, elephants can live to the ripe old age of 70, which is plenty of time to store up a lot of useful information.

Elephants use their memories to survive. Their great size means they need large quantities of food and water. They must remember where these resources can be found at certain times of year. Elephants use paths to remember how to reach their food sources. These paths are followed by herds for generations.

In India during the 1950s, a house was built over an elephant path. Every year the people who lived in the house had to fight off dozens of elephants who tried to walk right through the walls. One year the elephants actually knocked the house down to regain access to their path.

The elephants in a herd are usually female. Males tend to wander off by themselves. It is important for the herd's safety that the older females remember these males. and whether they are friendly or not. This enables them to mate to produce more young and to protect those young from possible danger.

Studies have shown that elephants can remember human beings. too. They can recognize an individual person, by sight or by scent, even when they have not met for decades.

There is even evidence that elephants can bear grudges against people. In 1929 in Texas, Black Diamond, an elephant in a traveling circus, killed a woman. People found out that the previous year when the circus had visited town, the woman had encouraged Black Diamond's trainer to run away from the circus. They suspected that the elephant had neither forgotten nor forgiven her.

Recently some experts have suggested that elephants' memories are so vivid that traumas during their infancy can cause them long-term suffering. As a result, their personalities can change. Basically they can turn into "teenage delinquents." For example, in the 1980s, in parts of Uganda, Africa, many elephants were slaughtered for their valuable ivory tusks. Some experts believe that as a result, hooligan elephants have been terrorizing road users and even attacking towns and villages in revenge attacks ever since.

WHY CAN'T I TASTE THINGS PROPERLY WHEN I HOLD MY NOSE?

You were born with about 10,000 taste buds in your mouth. Most of these are found on the surface of your tongue, and can detect sweet, savory, sour, bitter, and salty flavors.

Each of the taste buds on your tongue contains very sensitive microscopic hairlike filaments. These identify what you are eating and send information about it to your brain. They help you to survive by identifying bad or poisonous foods before you swallow them.

However, to taste complex flavors, such as nut-and-raisin chocolate or pepperoni pizza, your body needs lots more information, and this is where your nose comes in. When you tuck into the cheesy-meaty-tomatoeyness of a Deep Pan Supreme, you are actually smelling as well as tasting it.

It's not just your nose that gathers flavor information; there are receptors in your throat and even on the surface of your eyes that receive information, too. If you don't believe this, peel an onion and see how quickly your eyes begin to water.

If you hold your nose, you will keep air from reaching some of these receptors. This air is carrying all those flavor clues that fill out the complicated description of what you are eating. As a result, the "flavor picture" becomes more vague. You might be able to tell whether something is bitter, sweet, savory, salty, or sour, but anything much more complicated won't get through to your brain.

So pinch your nose and discover how hard it is for you to tell the difference between an apple and a pear, or even an apple and an onion. As for a Deep Pan Supreme, you might as well eat a slice of warm doormat!

DO CATS ALWAYS LAND ON THEIR FEET?

It is true that cats are remarkably skilled at correcting themselves in midair during a fall so that they land safely on the ground feetfirst. Maybe this is why some people say that cats seem to have nine lives.

However, doesn't this make you wonder why, if it is so agile, a cat ever falls in the first place? A cat is a hunter and, as a result, excellent at climbing trees. It has curved claws, which, as well as being useful weapons, are great for gripping things, climbing, running, and changing direction quickly when chasing lunch—whether that lunch is a bird, a mouse, or anything else that is tasty and running away. A cat is focused on its prey, so focused that it can occasionally tumble over, bump into things, or even fall out of a tree. When this happens, a cat's claws can act as a safety feature—grabbing on to passing branches to stop or slow down the fall.

A cat living on the tenth floor of an apartment building can easily become distracted when chasing a moth or a fly around a balcony, and it may fall over the edge. Modern buildings, unlike trees, tend to be made of smooth materials, such as glass and concrete, that are a lot harder to grab hold of in the event of a fall.

Is that the end of the cat? Not necessarily. Veterinarians in New York City have discovered that cats falling from high-rise buildings have a remarkably good survival rate. The strange thing is that the survival rate actually gets better if cats fall from a height *above* six floors up!

Why? Because while falling, a cat twists its body into a position where its feet are pointing downward and its legs are spread wide. Once it achieves this position, its body is acting a bit like a parachute. The cat stops accelerating and starts to relax, which helps it to absorb the impact on landing.

For the record, a cat takes about 3 feet (1 m) to turn itself the right way up when falling. Falls from heights greater than 3 feet often result in a cat landing feetfirst. Therefore, a cat falling from only one floor up is more likely to run out of time to turn, land awkwardly, and hurt itself than a cat falling from six floors up.

Records show that cats have fallen from more than 40 stories up and lived. The parachute effect means that a cat will achieve a maximum speed of around 59 miles (95 km) per hour—which is only about half the maximum speed a human being's body would reach if it fell from the same height.

This doesn't mean *all* cats live after a fall from 40 floors up. They don't. However, their instincts and their agility give them a good chance of surviving.

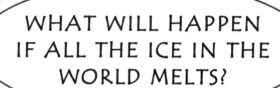

WHAT WILL HAPPEN IF ALL THE ICE IN THE WORLD MELTS?

Currently 65% to 70% of the world's fresh water is ice, held in glaciers and giant ice sheets. As this ice melts, the water flows into seas and oceans, and water levels rise around the world. But what will happen if all the ice melts?

Scientists overwhelmingly agree that Earth is getting warmer. Most scientists believe that the pollution human beings create is increasing the

speed at which the planet is heating up. Glaciers and ice sheets are melting. Over the next century, it is estimated that most of the world's mountain glaciers will disappear. This is of immediate concern because the people and animals who live near them will suffer flooding and, when the glaciers are gone, they will lose valuable water supplies. However, the levels of the planet's oceans will increase by only about 20 inches (.5 m).

There is a huge amount of ice at the North and South Poles of the Earth. In the north is the Arctic— a huge ocean of ice. Some scientists estimate that a 36°F (2°C) rise in water temperatures would be enough to melt much of the ice at the Arctic. They predict that in just 60 years there will be no ice

over the North Pole at all during the warmer summer months. This would affect all sorts of things, including marine life and global weather. However, it would not lead to the land being flooded. Think of the Arctic ice like ice cubes in a glass of water. If the ice cubes melt, the level of the water remains the same. So if the Arctic turned from ice into water, the water level would stay pretty much the same.

At the South Pole is the continent of Antarctica. It is made up of a massive sheet of ice lying on top of land, above the level of the sea. If the ice of Antarctica melts, the water created would pour off the land and into the sea. This would raise water levels all around the world. The rise could be as much as 198 feet (60 m). As a result, vast areas of the world, including most of its major cities, would disappear under water.

Fortunately, the Antarctic ice lies on top of rocks, and the rising temperature of the ocean around these rocks will not affect the ice immediately. It would take a much greater global temperature rise of approximately 50°F (10°C) or more to cause a serious melt. Currently experts agree that Antarctica is unlikely to melt for tens of thousands of years.

The giant ice sheet that covers the island of Greenland is thought to be melting faster than the ice at the Antarctic. More than 48 cubic miles (200 cu km) of ice is turning into water each year—imagine a cube 124 miles by 124 miles by 124 miles (200 km by 200 km by 200 km)—huge. If the whole Greenland ice sheet melted, the sea levels might rise by around 23 feet (7 m). This rise would threaten low-lying coastal regions and cause serious flooding problems in cities like London, Amsterdam, New York, Miami, New Orleans, Sydney, Bombay, Tokyo, and Rio de Janeiro, to name but a few.

But don't panic. There are some indications that while some of the Greenland ice sheet is melting, other areas of it are believed to be getting thicker.

CAN A HEADLESS CHICKEN RUN AROUND?

Have you ever been accused of running around like a headless chicken—making a lot of noise but not getting anything done? Surely a chicken without a head doesn't do an awful lot of running around.

Some insects, including hardy cockroaches, can survive for weeks with no heads, but then roaches breathe through their bodies and can go for weeks without food. Chickens can't. Most chickens that are separated from their heads simply die.

This fact is what makes Mike the Headless Chicken so remarkable. In 1945, in Fruita, Colorado, Mike the chicken had a date with the dinner table. Lloyd Olsen was given the job of finishing off the rooster with an ax so that his mom could serve Mike with potatoes and gravy.

By the time he died, Mike was famous around the world. He had lived for 18 months with no head— roosting, climbing, and, of course, running around like a headless chicken. It appears that Lloyd had not done a great job chopping off Mike's head, and enough of the bird's brain stem (the part of the

brain that runs down the neck connecting it to the spinal column) remained undamaged. This allowed Mike to pretty much carry on as normal.

Many people thought that the rumor of Mike's remarkable existence was a hoax. So Lloyd took the chicken to the University of Utah, and experts carried out a thorough examination. They confirmed that Mike was, indeed, headless and moreover, that he seemed happy.

Lloyd fed Mike milk and corn through the top of his neck with an eye-dropper. At the height of Mike's fame, Lloyd made around $5,000 a month showing him to paying visitors. Today Fruita still celebrates Mike the Headless Chicken Day every May.

Next time someone says you are running around like a headless chicken, think of Mike and be proud.

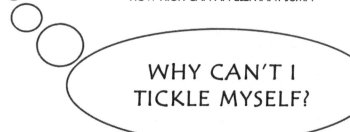

WHY CAN'T I TICKLE MYSELF?

If someone came up behind you and grabbed you, you would probably flinch or jump. This is because you have been taken by surprise and an area of your brain called the *cerebellum* hasn't been able to warn you of the attack.

One of the many jobs your cerebellum has is to predict when something is going to touch you. However suddenly you try to grab yourself, you won't

jump, because your brain knows exactly where your hand is and what it is doing, and it anticipates the sensation of being grabbed.

This is the reason that you can't tickle yourself. Part of the helpless feeling that comes with being tickled is a result of not knowing exactly when and where the tickle is going to happen.

Tickling studies have been carried out by scientists. Robots were programmed to copy the movements of a person's hand, simultaneously and exactly. If a person wired up to the robot moved their hand forward, the robot would move its hand forward in exactly the same way and at exactly the same moment. Tests showed that if the person made the movement to tickle themselves and the robot tickled them at exactly the same time, the tickle didn't work. However, if there was a delay, even a small one, between the tickling movement and the robot's action, the person got tickled.

Does that count as tickling yourself? You decide.

WHY DO KANGAROOS HOP?

In the drier areas of Australia, kangaroos often need to travel great distances in search of food and water. During these journeys, it is important that they conserve as much energy as possible—so they hop.

For human beings, hopping is not a very efficient way of getting around—but kangaroos are in a different league when it comes to hopping. When landing from a hop, energy is stored in the large, stretchy tendons in a kangaroo's hind legs and tail.

The tendons act like springs and release the energy again when the kangaroo takes off for the next hop.

Hops are useful to a kangaroo in other ways. The movement of the organs inside its body actually help it to breathe. Air is pushed in and out of its lungs as it bounces along. As a result, a kangaroo uses less energy breathing when it is at full hop than it does when it is standing still.

Scientists have studied kangaroos in motion on powered treadmills. They discovered that over short distances kangaroos can cruise along at speeds of 25 miles (40 km) per hour. At full sprint kangaroos can reach hopping speeds of up to 43 miles (70 km) per hour—as fast as a racehorse. However, when they want to speed up, kangaroos don't increase the

number of hops per minute by hopping faster; they make bigger hops. When a kangaroo is hopping at full speed, it can cover a distance of 30 feet (9 m) in one hop. There is an unconfirmed report that one particular kangaroo covered a distance of 43 feet (13 m) in one hop.

The scientists' studies showed that this method of speeding up by increasing the length of a hop is extremely efficient. It requires a fraction of the energy increase other animals need to switch from a jog to a sprint.

Kangaroos have few natural predators, but the hop is a great way of avoiding pursuing hunters—it's not easy to catch something that spends most of its time in the air and can clear rocks and rivers in a single bound.

HOW LONG COULD I SURVIVE BY EATING MYSELF?

If you were stranded somewhere with no food, could you survive until you were rescued by chopping off one of your legs and eating it? It is not a very pleasant thought, but certain animals, such as insects, mice, and sharks, have been known to eat bits of themselves when they are really hungry. Is it a good idea?

Archaeologists have found evidence that suggests people who lived 100,000 years ago ate one another, and some believe this gruesome practice was widespread. This suggests there is nothing deadly or poisonous about eating human flesh.

But what about eating yourself? There are a few problems with lopping off a leg and eating it. First and most obviously you wouldn't have a leg anymore. Second the pain and shock of the injury might kill you. Moreover your body might use up energy trying to heal the injury. In fact, your body would use as much energy healing the wound as it would gain from eating the leg.

You might think it would be a good idea to eat the parts of your body that you wouldn't miss and that would grow back, such as your hair or fingernails. The bad news is that there is very little energy-giving food to be had in these snacks. Nibbling the skin around your nails might provide a tiny bit of nourishment, but nothing you could really live on.

How about drinking your own blood? You could make a little nick in your arm that wouldn't hurt too much. Stories would have you believe that vampires drink blood, and some foods, such as black pudding, are actually made with animal blood. The problem with drinking your own blood is that blood is quite salty and drinking it will make you dehydrate (lose water in your body). In a survival situation, water is much more important to you than food. You can survive for weeks without food, but only a few days without water.

The reason you are so good at surviving without food is that after a couple of days without food your body starts to "eat" itself. It uses itself as fuel. Your body begins to burn up reserves of fat, and when that is gone, it will burn muscle. This is by far the most efficient way of surviving by eating yourself—and you'll still have both legs free to go and look for the nearest supermarket.

WHEN WILL THE SUN STOP BURNING?

The sun provides Earth with warmth and light. Without it, our planet would be just another frozen rock flying through space, with no plants, animals, or people to make it the interesting place it is.

The sun is a massive ball of gas. It gives off a huge amount of light and heat. This energy is released when hydrogen gas is turned into helium gas. This process is called *fusion*. It's a fantastically efficient way of creating energy. Scientists hope to use fusion to run power stations in years to come.

The sun is thought to be around five billion years old. As it uses up the hydrogen it contains, it will become bigger and brighter. As it grows, the sun will destroy the planet Mercury, and other planets, including Earth, will become burned-out rocks.

How long will this take? Scientists think the sun contains enough hydrogen to keep on burning for another five billion years. In one billion years the Earth may not be a place that anyone would want to live, but then, a billion years is a very, very long time. Even you won't be around then.

WHY DON'T WE RIDE ZEBRAS?

People have tried to tame and ride zebras for centuries. There are plenty of examples of zebras being trained to ride, pull carriages, and even jump fences. However, the simple answer to the question "Why don't we ride zebras?" is that they just don't like it.

Physically zebras are quite different from horses. Their backs are an awkward shape for a saddle. Their necks are strong but very stiff. They also don't have the same temperament as horses. They frighten easily, don't like doing what they are told, and can be bad tempered, even violent, on occasion.

In the 1900s, it became fashionable to use zebras to pull carts and carriages. On the plus side, they looked nice and were not affected by some of the diseases that killed mules and horses (most notably a disease called *nagana*, which is carried by a fly called the tsetse fly). On the down side, they didn't have the strength or stamina of mules, and although getting them to wear a harness was relatively simple, they generally took a lot longer to train.

Attempts to breed zebras with horses or donkeys have been successful. The results (called, naturally enough, zorses and zonkeys) were healthy, but as domestic working animals they were no more useful than normal horses and donkeys.

A movie called *Racing Stripes* told the story of a zebra in a circus who dreamed of being a champion racehorse. Eleven real zebras were used in the making of the film, and each was trained to perform different circus tricks. According to the movie's animal handler, Steve Martin, zebras are a lot easier to train if you start when they are babies.

Can a zebra run faster than a horse? Well, a zebra can reach speeds of up to 34 miles (55 km) per hour in a shortish sprint (particularly if it is being chased by a lion). Zebras are particularly good at changing direction while moving very fast. However, over a longer distance, in a straight line, a horse would probably win.

WHY ARE YAWNS SO CONTAGIOUS?

It has probably happened to you—one hour into a long history lesson on a rainy Tuesday afternoon someone yawns. Before you know it the whole class is at it. Why?

The problem when answering this question is that no one is really sure why yawns happen at all. One theory is that you yawn to wake yourself up and

more alert. You'll have noticed that ~~wn~~ when you are sleepy (or bored in ~~~s~~). Stretching and yawning increases ~~~ssure~~ and your heart rate, both of which make your body more alert. Moreover, your brain might decide you are feeling dopey because there is not enough oxygen in your blood—in which case taking in a big breath of air with a yawn would certainly seem a sensible thing to do.

If this is the case, yawns might be a very useful survival mechanism. After all, someone who is half asleep is more likely to be eaten by a polar bear than someone who is wide awake. This would then explain why yawns are contagious. When you watch other people yawn, your brain may subconsciously tell you that people around you are preparing to face danger and that you should probably start preparing, too— just in case.

Did you know that yawns are even contagious between different animals? (Try yawning in front of your cat; more than likely you will set him off.) In fact, yawns are so contagious that even looking at and thinking about the word *yawn* can get you yawning.

Well, has it?

WHAT SHOULD I DO IF I'M MAROONED ON A DESERT ISLAND?

The obvious answer to the question "What should I do if I'm marooned on a desert island?" is—get rescued. However, it may take months, and though there are things you can do to make rescue more likely, your immediate problem is keeping yourself alive. You don't want to be just a skeleton lying on the beach when a helicopter does turn up.

The necessities for human survival are water, food, fire, and shelter. You need all four to survive for any length of time. Believe it or not, a healthy human being can survive for more than 40 days without food. Unfortunately, after a few days of missed meals, you will feel weak and find it difficult to think straight. Your body will become more vulnerable to diseases and less able to mend itself if injured. But you won't die.

Water is far more important than food. You can survive only about three days without it. The amount of water your body loses depends on how active you are and how hot you get, but it must be replaced or you will suffer dehydration, headaches, dizziness, and confusion. Without water you will be pretty useless and eventually die.

You might think that on an island surrounded by an ocean, finding water wouldn't be a problem. However, any water you drink must be fresh, clean, and free from salt, so drinking seawater is out. If you can't find fresh water on your island, rainwater will do. You can collect rainwater in a container or, failing that, use a piece of material to soak up dew from plants in the mornings.

A fire will keep you warm and keep dangerous animals at bay. More important, you can use it to

boil any water that you find on the island. This will kill many of the things contaminating the water that could make you sick. You can also use your fire to cook any food you find. Another important function of your fire would be to signal ships and aircraft by using its light and smoke.

Some specialists put building a shelter at the top of their list of things to do in a survival situation. A simple shelter that keeps you dry and protected from the sun and the weather will enable you to sleep. This means you will conserve the energy you need to hunt and gather supplies and plan your escape.

DO DOLPHINS TALK TO EACH OTHER?

Dolphins do communicate with each other. They use two kinds of sound signal, known by scientists as *clicks* and *whistles*. For the most part, these signals can't be heard by human beings, so scientists use special equipment to record and study them.

Dolphins appear to use clicks to locate objects. A dolphin sends out a loud click and hears an echo when it bounces off something. The echo gives the dolphin information about the location of the object and builds up a kind of "sound map." This technique is known as *echolocation*.

Dolphins appear to use whistles to identify other dolphins and call to them. Each dolphin seems to make his or her own personal whistle like a unique signature. They can also imitate the whistles of other dolphins. They will imitate another dolphin's whistle to call out to it, a bit like shouting someone's name to get their attention.

A dolphin's signature whistle develops quite early in its life, and seems to be a close copy of its mother's

42

personal whistle. So there is a resemblance between the whistles of family members. Scientists studying groups of dolphins (called *pods*) have discovered that dolphins can communicate the presence of danger, or the location of food. These messages can be passed from one dolphin to another, sometimes over great distances, so that everyone in the pod gets the news.

Scientists have also shown that dolphins can pass on more complicated messages. An experiment was set up in which a dolphin had to press a series of buttons in a particular sequence, using its nose to release food—the dolphin was able to successfully communicate the correct sequence to another dolphin.

Many trained dolphins have been able to understand sign language, and some have been able to understand spoken words. Some experts believe that dolphins can even be trained to understand whole sentences, such as "Hit the ball and then jump through the hoop."

Some scientists think that dolphins have "words" for things and use them to communicate with each other—it has even been suggested that one pod of dolphins might have a language or accent different from that of another pod.

No studies have yet proved that dolphins have actual conversations with each other, but the full range of their language skills is still being studied. More discoveries are being made all the time. Maybe one day scientists might be able to translate what dolphins are saying—and even talk back to them.

IS CHOCOLATE REALLY BAD FOR ME?

Too much of anything is usually bad for you, and chocolate is no different. You probably know that eating chocolate all the time harms your teeth because of all the sugar it contains. It might also give you pimples, and large quantities will eventually make you fat.

Chocolate contains a chemical called *theobromine*, which humans can digest safely. However, many animals, especially cats and dogs, cannot digest it. Theobromine can stay in an animal's body for up to 20 hours and is poisonous. Even a small amount of chocolate, 2 ounces (50 g) or so, is extremely harmful to a dog or cat and could even kill them.

Theobromine is also harmful to babies and very young children. Their bodies are less able to process the chemical than the bodies of older kids and adults. That's one reason why small children who binge on chocolate get sick. So now you have the perfect excuse to take chocolate away from your kid brother or sister—you are being kind and merciful.

But chocolate is not all bad news ... There are about 380 known chemicals in chocolate, and some of them are actually good for you.

There are collections of chemicals in cocoa beans called *flavonoids* that may help to keep clots from forming in human blood and reduce the risk of heart attacks.

Chocolate has been found to have a soothing effect on coughs.

Scientists are investigating whether drugs made using cocoa beans could help people with diabetes. Chocolate contains ingredients that may make you feel happier by making your brain release mood-improving chemicals.

A little bit of pure, dark chocolate can make your skin better. Studies have shown that it is the fats in milk chocolate bars that cause acne, not the cocoa.

So could chocolate kill you? Well, if you ate enough chocolate at one time, you might flood your body with enough toxins to cause fatal poisoning. The amount it would take to do this would be less if you are small rather than tall and much, much less if you are a cat ... But don't worry, Kitty: Any cat reading this book is probably smart enough to know that already.

HOW MANY SPECIES OF ANIMAL ARE STILL UNDISCOVERED?

There are currently about one and a half million different species of animal known to us. Different scientists give very different estimates of how many species remain undiscovered on our planet. Their estimates range from half a million to 50 million. The truth is no one knows exactly how many species remain undiscovered.

A ten-year-long census of marine life has been under way since 2003. Three hundred of the world's marine biologists are logging all the species of fish known to them. These scientists believe that by the time the census has finished, in 2013, they will have found 5,000 new species of fish, raising the total number of known species of fish to 20,000.

Logging species of fish is one thing, but recording all the different insects on Earth is an altogether bigger task. More than half of all the species currently recorded are insects, including approximately 300,000 beetles. Some estimates put the total of different insect species at more than 30 million,

yet less than one million different species have been documented up to now.

Based on current research, it would be fair to say that a new species of fish is discovered about three times a week. But what about a new beetle? In the Amazon rain forest, pretty much anyone with a matchbox and a magnifying glass has a good chance of finding a new species of beetle before breakfast!

In comparison, only about 4,500 mammals are known to exist, so if a new one is discovered, you can't blame scientists for getting very excited.

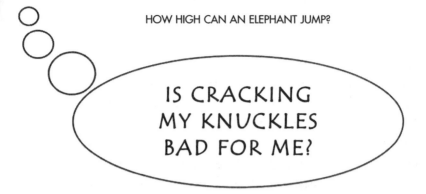

IS CRACKING MY KNUCKLES BAD FOR ME?

Have you ever been fussed at for cracking your knuckles? Has someone winced and warned you that you are causing terrible damage to your hands? Perhaps you thought the only reason they were complaining was that they hated the ghastly double-crunching noise your knuckles make.

The space between your finger bones in each of your knuckle joints is filled with a liquid called *synovial fluid.* This helps to lubricate the joint and

keep it working smoothly. On either side of the knuckle joint are *ligaments*, which are tough strings of tissue that hold your joints and bones together. When you crack your knuckle joint, you are stretching the joint and making the space between your finger bones bigger. This causes bubbles of gas to form in the synovial fluid. The popping sound is caused by the bubbles popping.

But is cracking your knuckles actually harmful? Well, joint injuries often involve tearing *cartilage*. Cartilage is the tough, gristly tissue that forms a kind of cushion between bones. Cracking your knuckles puts the cartilage under some stress, but probably not enough to cause damage.

Studies on people who have been cracking their knuckles regularly for a long time show that they have slightly swollen knuckle joints compared with non-crackers. What is more concerning is that these people have a grip that is significantly weaker than it should be. This suggests that habitual knuckle-cracking might make your hands weaker over time.

So if you crack your knuckles—stop now.

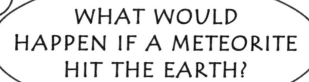

WHAT WOULD HAPPEN IF A METEORITE HIT THE EARTH?

A meteorite is a lump of rock, iron, or other material flying through space. Millions enter the Earth's atmosphere every year, but most are so small that they burn away to nothing. Sometimes you will see them burning up—they are called shooting stars.

Dust from burned-up meteorites is constantly falling to Earth, but the number of meteorites bigger than the size of a marble that survive the fiery fall is nearer to five hundred a year.

The biggest meteorite ever found on Earth is the Hoba meteorite, which astronomers estimate landed 80,000 years ago in Namibia, Africa. A lot of the Hoba meteorite has rusted away since it landed on Earth, but it still weighs about 60 tons. Experts believe that the Earth's atmosphere slowed down the meteorite as it fell, so it landed pretty much in one piece and didn't cause a huge crater.

Few meteorites are big enough to cause a crater in the Earth's surface. However, if a very large meteorite entered our atmosphere, it wouldn't slow down much. It would thump into the ground at an incredible speed, at least 24,000 miles (40,000 km) per hour or faster. This would make a huge crater and kick up millions of tons of burning debris. The debris would set fire to anything it came into contact with.

The shockwave from the meteorite's impact would flatten everything for miles around. The dust thrown into the air by the impact of the meteorite may also cause the sunlight to be blocked out for weeks or even years. If a meteorite this size landed in the ocean, it would create huge waves that would cause devastating floods in coastal areas.

Many scientists believe that a large meteorite (about 6 miles [10 km] in diameter) smashing into the Earth killed off the dinosaurs millions of years ago. They think that a hole 112-miles (180-km) wide near the Mexican coast was caused by a massive impact. The hole is called the Chicxulub crater. Chicxulub is a Maya word meaning "the tail of the devil." The dust from the impact blocked out the sun for many years. Plants stopped growing because of the lack of sunlight. This left nothing for the dinosaurs to eat and led to their extinction.

The good news is that a meteorite as big as the one that caused the Chicxulub crater turns up only about once every 100 million years. Another good thing is that the world's astronomers who study space would probably see it approaching Earth from a long way off. They are constantly searching the galaxy for giant meteorites on a collision course with our planet.

If astronomers did spot a meteorite that they calculated would collide with Earth in 10 or 20 years' time, they would need to decide how to prevent this disaster. Different methods of doing this have been suggested. One way might be to nudge the meteorite off its collision course, either by attaching a huge sail to it or using the explosion of a nuclear weapon. This would be tricky, because meteorites are spinning all the time, making them hard to control. Also, a meteorite the size of Mount Everest would not be easy to push around.

Another method of preventing collision might be to blow the meteorite to pieces before it gets here. This is a risky idea, because the effect of millions of big rocks entering the planet's atmosphere could be almost as disastrous as the effect of one enormous one.

AM I MORE LIKELY TO BE EATEN BY A SHARK, A LION, OR A CROCODILE?

The short answer to this question is that approximately 10 people are killed by sharks each year, whereas as many as 700 people are killed by crocodiles, and about the same number by lions and tigers. The difference is that crocodiles are the most likely to *want* to eat you.

The reason that fatal shark attacks are relatively few and far between may be because humans don't generally "live" in the sea, so they don't bump into sharks very often. Of the approximately 400 species of sharks out there, only 4 or 5 are dangerous to humans. Sharks don't seem to hunt people on purpose. They are more likely to nibble people, mistaking them for big fishes or seals. They would probably stop once they realized what they were eating. Unfortunately, a nibble from a shark is sometimes fatal, with people dying from the shock of the attack. In fact, sharks have much more to fear from humans, who kill millions of sharks every year.

Lions and tigers don't consider humans prey, and rarely seek them out for attack. Some people believe

that an old or injured lion, unable to hunt its normal prey, will hunt people out of necessity. Once a lion has killed and eaten a human, it is likely he (and man-eating lions usually are male) will do it again. There have been cases of single lions or tigers that have developed a taste for people and have gone on to kill dozens, or even hundreds, over a period of years. In Tanzania in the 1940s, a pride of lions turned man-eaters, and killed 1,500 people.

Crocodiles are different. Any croc big enough to attack and eat you will do it without a second thought. A crocodile's bite can be ten times more powerful than that of a big shark. They are "ambush hunters" and hide themselves in water or behind a bush, waiting for something to wander up close. Then they attack.

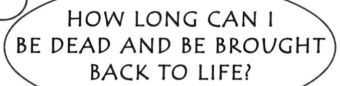

HOW LONG CAN I
BE DEAD AND BE BROUGHT
BACK TO LIFE?

A person who is dead, whose heart has stopped beating, can be brought back to life. Their heart can often be restarted by applying an electric shock, and their body can begin to function again.

If this *resuscitation* happens within five minutes of someone's heart stopping, there is a good chance that they will make a full recovery. If a longer period of time passes (more than eight minutes), a person's brain will have been deprived of oxygen and may well have suffered permanent damage.

Doctors have found that some people who have almost drowned in very cold water can make a good recovery, even if they have been under water for 30 minutes or more. Someone plunging into cold water experiences a *diving response*. This means their body reacts to the cold water by reducing the blood supply to the skin and muscles and supplying more blood to the heart and brain. As a result, these organs continue to receive vital oxygen for longer. The younger a person is, the better their chances are of surviving.

Cryonics is the practice of using extreme cold (minus 266°F [130°C]) and chemicals to preserve the bodies of people who can't be kept alive by current medicine. The idea is that someone who has died of a disease, a medical condition, or of old age can be frozen and stored. Then at some time in the future, when medicine has progressed, it might be possible to defrost, resuscitate, and cure them. Around the world more than a hundred people are currently being stored using cryonics, and thousands more have made arrangements to be preserved in this way.

No one has yet been brought back to life after being cryopreserved. It may be hundreds of years before medicine and technology is advanced enough to try.

WHAT IS THE RAREST ANIMAL IN THE WORLD?

The most endangered any animal can be is when only one example of it remains. Unless another creature of the same species (and of the opposite sex) comes along, that species is pretty much doomed to become extinct.

Thylacines, or Tasmanian tigers, have been officially extinct since 1936. These creatures actually look more like stripy wild dogs than tigers. The last known thylacine, named Benjamin, died in Hobart Zoo on the island of Tasmania, Australia. Benjamin

(who may actually have been a female) remains the last one ever seen alive. Therefore, at that time, it could have been the only thylacine left in the world.

There have been investigations and expeditions, and a research and data center was opened, dedicated to finding thylacines. Since Benjamin died, there have been more than 300 reported sightings of thylacines, but none has ever been verified as genuine.

"Lonesome George" is a Pinta Island tortoise. In 1972 he was taken to live in the Charles Darwin Research Station on Santa Cruz island in the eastern Pacific Ocean. Until George was discovered, the species was thought to have been hunted to extinction. The *Guinness Book of World Records* names George as the world's rarest living creature.

The research scientists have offered a reward to anyone who finds a female Pinta Island tortoise. Sadly none has been found. George refuses to mate with any other species of the giant tortoise, so unless a female is found, he may end up being the last of his kind.

In 1997, a single male example of a newly discovered species of lizard, the Coromandel striped gecko, was found in the town of Coromandel, New Zealand. It was kept in captivity for four years, but died before anyone could find a female. Too late, a female was located, and the search began for another male. Sadly, the female was attacked by a bird and passed away from her injuries before a male was found.

In 2007, a male Coromandel striped gecko turned up, just 330 yards (300 m) away from where the original gecko had been found. Now the search is back on for a female. If one isn't found soon, the male will be electronically tagged and released into the wild to see if he is any better at locating a mate by himself. With just three examples ever recorded, but never two existing at the same time, the Coromandel striped gecko might well qualify as the world's rarest animal.

DO TWINS HAVE THE SAME FINGERPRINTS?

The difference between a pair of identical twins and a pair of non-identical twins is that the identical ones come from a single egg in their mother's womb. Non-identical ones come from separate eggs.

Non-identical twins are as similar to each other as brothers and sisters who are born at different times. They can have different colored eyes or hair and won't necessarily look like each other at all.

Identical twins are pretty much the same person, because they come from the same egg. They have exactly the same biological and chemical makeup. Their eye and hair color will be the same, and they tend to look *very* alike.

However, in the womb, once the egg that identical twins come from has split into two separate people, the twins can develop differently. Factors affect the babies in the womb that will lead to tiny differences developing before and after they are born. These factors include if the babies lie in different positions, if they face in different directions, and if they get different amounts of nourishment as they develop, which will cause them to grow at slightly different rates.

Identical twins might look very similar, but small details, such as the position of every hair on their heads and every freckle or mole on their bodies, vary.

Fingerprints fall into this category. A fingerprint is so detailed and complicated that each is unique to its owner. Even identical twins can be identified separately by their fingerprints, which will be similar, but not identical. So police at a crime scene would have little difficulty telling which of a pair of identical twins committed the crime . . .

WHY DON'T POLAR BEARS MOVE SOMEWHERE WARMER?

Polar bears are mainly found in cold northern regions near the North Pole, such as parts of Russia, Norway, Greenland, Canada, and Alaska. They like to live by the sea, where the ice melts in the summer and freezes again in the winter, and where the seals they love to eat live.

Some scientists suspect that about a quarter of a million years ago, some brown bears may have been trapped in the far north by winter ice. In order to survive, the bears would probably have had to adapt themselves to their harsh new environment. These adaptations would have taken place gradually.

Over many generations, the bears grew bigger. (Today adult male polar bears measure 8 to 12 feet [2.5 to 3.5 m] long and weigh 880 to 1,320 pounds [400 to 600 kg].) Their legs became very powerful and their paws thickly furred to enable them to climb and run on snow and ice. Their claws and teeth grew longer and sharper so they could hunt prey and eat meat.

In their new environment, the bears needed to be excellent swimmers, so their necks grew longer and their paws became slightly webbed.

Today polar bears have creamy-white fur, which is excellent for camouflaging them in their snowy environment. Polar bears also have a thick layer of blubber beneath their skin to keep them warm, which is just as well for creatures that have to survive in the harsh conditions of the Arctic, where winter temperatures can plunge to minus 113°F (45°C).

Today, polar bears are incredibly well suited to survive in the places they live. They are the most feared and effective predators in their part of the world. Polar bears have no real competition for food in the polar regions, and nothing is big enough and powerful enough to enjoy polar bears for dinner.

Moving to the warmer south might mean polar bears could live in a less harsh environment, but it would also mean living among other large predators, such as other bears, big cats, wolves, and even crocodiles.

Polar bears would have to compete with these creatures for available food, and they would probably have to protect their cubs from them, too.

The characteristics that polar bears have developed
to cope with the sea ice of their homeland are not
suited to a warmer environment. Their creamy-white
fur would make them so easy to spot that any prey
would see them a mile off and have time to escape.
This, of course would make dinner very difficult to
catch. Moreover, polar bears' long, flesh-tearing teeth
are no longer any good for chewing plants.

So, though it might seem a good idea for polar
bears to pack their bags and move to Florida,
they really are better off where they live now.
A barren landscape of ice and snow might seem
pretty unpleasant, but for polar bears it's home
sweet home.

WHAT MAKES THE NOISE OF THUNDER?

Don't believe anyone who tells you the sound of thunder is caused by "clouds bumping into each other." Smile sympathetically and walk away.

Lightning strikes somewhere on Earth a hundred times every second. The huge release of electricity that occurs during a bolt of lightning heats the air around it to about 54,000°F (30,000°C). Heated air expands, and the air around the bolt becomes instantly squashed. As a result, the air pressure around the bolt increases a hundredfold, causing it to explode outward, sending shockwaves in all directions. This is what makes the big booming noise.

Light travels more quickly than sound, so you will see the flash of lightning before you hear the thunder. A single vertical bolt of lightning will produce a single bang, but the shockwaves will reach you gradually, in one long rumble, starting with the ones near the ground that are nearest to you and ending with the ones coming at you from the top of the bolt.

Forked lightning consists of many different bolts, and the shockwaves from all the different strikes will bounce off each other and make low rumbling thunder that goes on for a long time.

Occasionally, no thunder accompanies a lightning bolt. This is thought to happen when a bolt travels more slowly than normal, giving the heated air around the bolt time to expand more gradually rather than exploding.

WHAT MAKES SOMEONE PRETTY?

Everyone has different tastes when it comes to who they find most attractive and whose picture they will pin up on their wall and drool over. Just ask your friends who they like and you will see. However, people tend to agree on whether someone is pretty or ugly.

Some studies suggest that one of the most important things in being attractive is *symmetry*. If someone's looks are described as symmetrical, it means one side of their body and face looks very similar to the other side. Most people have differences between one side and the other. Take a look at yourself. You might have slightly different sized feet, one leg a bit longer than the other, one eyebrow higher up than the other one, or teeth that don't match on both sides.

Often small differences in the symmetry of a body and face are caused by illnesses or injuries, or occur as a result of damage during birth. For this reason people's brains may associate a symmetrical body and face with a strong, healthy person. When human beings are looking for someone to have

70

children with, they want a strong, healthy partner who is more likely to provide healthy children. This is important because healthy children are more likely to ensure the survival of a species.

This love of symmetry has been observed in other animals, too. One scientist found that clipping the tail feathers of male swallows with scissors to make their tail less symmetrical dramatically reduced the birds' attractiveness to females. Another scientist discovered that bees tend to prefer symmetrical flowers. If petals were removed from one side of the flowers, for example, the bees were less attracted to them.

There is a lot more to prettiness than symmetry, but if you are fairly confident your face is symmetrical, that's cool—just watch out for bees!

WHICH ARE SMARTER— CATS OR DOGS?

It's difficult to measure intelligence between one human being and another, let alone between two completely different species of animal. Different people have different skills—for example, a rocket scientist might be hopeless at writing poetry. So when answering the question "Which are smarter—cats or dogs?" their different skills need to be considered.

Dogs are easier to train than cats. This is because they prefer to live in packs and have developed greater social skills than their feline friends. A pack of dogs must work together and communicate to hunt successfully. When you own a dog, it usually considers you the boss and itself a member of your pack. Therefore it will try to please you by doing what you tell it.

Cats don't really care about pleasing others. They won't try to learn tricks just for your amusement. They naturally prefer to hunt alone. However, cats are better than dogs at solving problems, and at reasoning and learning by copying behavior they see in others. Cats have been known to learn how

72

to turn on taps, open cupboards, and even use the toilet, but usually because the cat is thirsty, hungry, or doesn't like the smell of poo! Cats are kind of selfish. This ability to learn by copying behavior has been shown in monkeys and cats, but not so much in dogs.

Dogs can recognize signals and verbal commands given by their owners, which helps them become excellent sheepherders, rescue dogs, guard dogs, police dogs, and guides for the blind. A dog's superior social skills also make it better at picking up on other forms of communication, such as a person's mood or body language. Some dogs seem able to detect illness—even undiagnosed cancer—in human beings.

Cats have been found to have greater navigational skills, and can remember what things look like longer than dogs. If you took a cat more than 19 miles (30 km) away from home and abandoned it, a week later it could well find its way home.

One approximate way to estimate the intelligence of an animal is to measure the weight of its brain in relation to its body. In the animal world, apes have the highest brain-to-body-weight ratio, followed by whales and dolphins, and then by cats. Dogs come way down the list.

It's a close call. Suffice to say that a smart dog is smarter than a dumb cat and vice versa. For the record, poodles are usually smarter than Afghan hounds, and Siamese cats are usually smarter than Persians.

WHY IS THE STUFF THAT TASTES GOOD BAD FOR ME?

Don't you just hate the way that the stuff you like to eat, such as pizza, sweets, and cheeseburgers, is usually bad for you, and the healthy foods—broccoli and brussels sprouts—taste awful? Have you ever asked yourself why you tend to like things that taste sweet or fatty—such as cheesecake and chips—and dislike stuff that tastes bitter, such as spinach or cabbage?

For hundreds of years scientists have divided basic tastes into sweet, sour, salty, and bitter. A fifth taste called *umami* was added around a hundred years ago. Umami is a kind of satisfying meaty, savory taste. To survive, human beings need sugar, salt, and protein in their diet, so maybe this is why they like the taste of sweet, salty, and meaty foods.

In nature, sweetness (and sometimes sourness) is often a clue that a food can be eaten safely and contains good things, such as vitamin C. Bitterness, on the other hand, is sometimes an indication that a food is poisonous and should be avoided. Young children (and pregnant mothers) instinctively steer clear of bitter-tasting foods, perhaps for this very reason.

According to research, *phytochemicals* found in some fruits and vegetables help your body combat diseases. Broccoli, cabbage, and sprouts are particularly strong in this area, but many people don't like to eat them because they can have a bitter taste. Food scientists worked hard to breed these healthy vegetables to taste nicer, so kids would eat more of them, but discovered that the very phytochemicals that make them good at combating disease also make them taste bitter! The sprouts that were bred to taste nicer turned out to have fewer of the good chemicals.

So in this case the answer is yes—the worse it tastes, the better it is for you!

WHY DO SQUIRRELS HAVE BUSHY TAILS?

Squirrels are rodents, and come from the same animal family as rats and mice, but unlike these cousins, squirrels have big bushy tails. There are many factors that make these tails more than just impressive fashion accessories.

Monkeys in trees use their tails for grabbing and swinging. Squirrels spend much of their time in trees but use their tails primarily to balance as they run along branches. When squirrels are standing still on a branch, the tails act like tightrope walkers'

77

poles, balancing with the squirrels' bodies and keeping them stable. If squirrels are unlucky enough to fall, their tails act as a kind of parachute, slowing their descent and making for a softer landing. Even on the ground, the big, bushy tails act like rudders when the squirrels run, and help them to change direction while running.

Squirrels' tails are as comfy and fluffy as they look. In the long winter months, when the temperature drops and food becomes more scarce, squirrels spend a lot of time curled up, using their tails as duvets, conserving heat and energy.

In the summer, squirrels can use their tails as protection from the sun—indeed the word *squirrel* derives from the Greek words *skia*, meaning "shadow," and *oura*, meaning "tail."

For defense, squirrels have some pretty impressive teeth to rely on, but their tails come in handy, too. First, their tails double the size of the squirrels, making them look bigger and scarier than they actually are. Second, the squirrels shelter under their tails when on the ground, using them as fluffy barriers that protect their bodies from birds of prey attacking from the sky. The tails give the birds nothing solid to grab hold of and easily slip through their talons.

Most remarkably, perhaps, squirrels have found a way of fending off rattlesnakes with their tails. Rattlesnakes use sensitive heat detectors on their heads to find prey. On encountering rattlers, squirrels heat up their tails (which are usually cool) by filling them with blood. Faced with a hot thrashing tail, most rattlesnakes back off and go elsewhere for lunch. Many scientists are convinced the squirrels' reaction is deliberate, because faced with other kinds of snakes that don't have heat sensors, they don't bother to heat up their tails. A specially constructed robot squirrel with a remote-controlled, heatable tail also proved effective at repelling a rattlesnake attack.

So, squirrels' tails turn out to be parasols, parachutes, rudders, balancing aids, duvets, shields, and rattlesnake deterrents! Oh, and it makes them look cute, too ... When was the last time you saw a rat on a greeting card?

ARE MY DREAMS TRYING TO TELL ME SOMETHING?

People dream on average for two hours each night. Scientists aren't sure why, or even exactly where in the brain dreams come from. Nor has anyone proved whether dreams have any meaning.

Some experts believe that the subjects of your dreams reveal your deepest wishes and emotions. Other scientists think dreams are just random images and thoughts in your sleeping head that the brain tries to make sense of by putting them into a story, and that they have no real meaning. Either way, it seems that the things you are dreaming about are important to you. If that is the case, maybe you should try to figure out what you are trying to tell yourself.

Oneirologists is the name given to people who try to *interpret* dreams, which means "explain what they mean." Some dreams are common to lots of people, and there is a fair amount of agreement among oneirologists about what they might mean.

Have you had any of the following dreams?

Being naked in a dream might mean that in real life you feel embarrassed about something, or that you have a secret you are worried about being revealed. Nakedness at school might suggest you don't feel prepared and are worried that people will find out and make fun of you.

Falling is a sign that you feel insecure, out of control, or that you've failed in some way. Often people will wake up with a jerk from a falling dream—but it certainly isn't true that if you hit the ground in your dream, you will die in real life!

Exam dreams indicate that you are being measured or tested in some way. If the dream exam is going badly, it might mean that you feel you aren't fitting in or being accepted, or that you are worried about letting someone down.

Flying in a dream may indicate that you feel on top of things and are seeing things clearly—unless you are flying out of control, in which case it could mean that you are afraid of challenges, or even of success and the extra pressure that comes with it.

Losing teeth is a very common and upsetting dream, but it can mean simply that you are growing and maturing in life, losing your "baby teeth" (or your childish ways).

Being chased in a dream might indicate that you are avoiding problems in your life, by running away from them rather than trying to solve them. The key to chase dreams is to figure out what or who is chasing you. It might look like a lion, but it could be your geography homework, or that conversation you have to have with Dad about losing your iPod . . .

If you want to remember a dream, lie very still when you wake up and allow yourself to remember it. Keep a piece of paper by the bed so you can write it down.

Are dreams trying to tell you something? Well, yes. At the very least they are telling you about your emotions and worries, some of which you might have been hiding from yourself. Maybe you try to make sense of your world in dreams. Dream interpretation certainly can make you look at your problems in a new way, and sometimes that might be just what you need to do.

HOW MUCH ROOM IS THERE ON EARTH FOR EACH PERSON?

Currently there are more than six and a half billion people on Earth. If you looked at pictures of people on the streets of Hong Kong, New York, or London, you could be forgiven for thinking that the world is a pretty crowded place. However, there are still plenty of places on Earth, such as Canada and Greenland, where vast amounts of land are occupied by only a few people.

The total surface area of Earth is 204 million square miles (510 million sq km). This works out at about 0.03 square miles (0.078 sq km) for each of the six and a half billion people on Earth. That's 858,000 square feet (78,000 sq m).

This might sound like quite a decent-sized piece of land. However, 70% of the Earth is covered in water, and a large proportion of the rest is covered in ice or desert. So these areas are not really somewhere people could live. Only about 10% of the Earth's surface can be successfully lived on. That is about 20.4 million square miles (51 million sq km) of inhabitable land. Divided between six and a half billion people, that gives each person about 85,800 square feet (7,800 sq m).

Some people don't get nearly that much space to roam. For example, the 35,000 people who live in Monaco (a tiny, crowded, but very wealthy country in the south of Europe) occupy on average just 704 square feet (64 sq m). Bear in mind that's a square measuring only 26 feet by 26 feet (8 m by 8 m).

WHAT COLOR ARE A ZEBRA'S STRIPES?

There are three species of zebra, all with the familiar black-and-white-stripy thing going on. The number of stripes ranges from 26 per side on a common zebra up to 80 stripes per side on an imperial zebra. But are zebras black with white stripes, or white with black stripes? It's a question that has caused many a fight between otherwise perfectly polite zoologists.

The case for black animals with white stripes is convincing. Very occasionally zebras are born with spots instead of stripes. These spots are always white on a black background, so it seems logical that the stripes are also white on a black background.

And there's more ... If you were to sneak up on a zebra while it was sleeping and shave off all its hair, the skin underneath would be black or dark brown.

But don't make your mind up yet ...

A zebra's black hairs are black because they contain cells that produce a dark pigment. When a baby

zebra starts to grow inside its mother, none of its hair cells produce this pigment, so it is completely white. The dark stripes appear only as the baby zebra grows, so it seems that the stripes are black on a white background.

Whichever side you're on, one thing everyone agrees on is that zebras have stripes to protect them from hungry lions. Lions are color-blind and the zebra's stripes make it difficult for lions to spot them amongst their natural habitat of tall grasses.

WHY DON'T SPIDERS STICK TO THEIR OWN WEBS?

All spiders make webs—some webs are big, some small, some neat and tidy, others completely messy. Not all spiderwebs are sticky. The ones that are, are made that way to trap insects for spiders to eat. A fly hits the web and becomes glued to it until the spider comes out and has it for lunch. But how can the spider move around on the web when the poor fly can't budge?

Spiderwebs are made from a substance commonly called silk. A spider can make different kinds of silk for different purposes. The silk they produce to wrap up eggs or to trap insects is different from the silk produced to make a web. Some silks are sticky and others are not.

To make a trapping web, a spider creates a web the shape of a bicycle wheel. First a single strand of silk is attached between two twigs of a tree. Then a rim, like the tire on a bicycle wheel, is spun in a circle around the outside, with a diameter the width of the space between the twigs. The "spokes" are added next, followed by a loose spiral running from the center of the web out to the rim. This forms the main structure of the web, and none of the silk used to make it is sticky.

Next, the spider weaves a second spiral over the web. This time the silk spun is coated with a sticky stuff that flies will get trapped in. When the web is finished, the spider knows exactly which silk strands are sticky and which are not. It walks on the spokes, spiral, and the rim of the web that aren't sticky, and avoids the spiral that is.

WHY IS THE SKY BLUE?

White light from the sun is made up of a mixture of the colors you would see in a rainbow. All these colors are in the form of waves. The reddish colors have long wavelengths, and bluish ones have shorter wavelengths.

The Earth's atmosphere contains atoms of nitrogen and oxygen. When light waves pass through it, they are scattered by these atoms. The reddish waves are scattered least and the bluish light is scattered most. Therefore most of the light that is scattered down to your eyes is bluish.

The sun looks yellow to you, because the light coming straight at your eyes from the sun has lost some of its blue because of scattering. When the sun sets and its light has to pass through more air to reach you, it changes from yellow to orange to red as more of the shorter-wavelength blue and green light is scattered and only the longer wavelength red light survives the journey to your eye.

The sky isn't always blue, though. Different weather and atmospheric conditions can make it appear different colors. It can sometimes look bright red. Particles of dust, water, volcanic ash, or pollution in the air can all affect the way the light behaves and change the color of the sky. The more particles there are in the air, the less of the short-wavelength light makes it to your eye, and the redder the sky will appear.

COULD SCIENTISTS EVER BRING DINOSAURS BACK TO LIFE?

Wouldn't it be great to have your very own pet triceratops stomping around the garden? Imagine how much stuff it could carry when you're coming back from shopping. Scientists have cloned sheep and cats, so why not dinosaurs?

First, they would need some dinosaur DNA. DNA is the information contained in all the cells of an animal that provides instructions telling it what to look like as it grows. But how would they find the DNA of an extinct creature?

Ideally, one day, millions of years ago, a mosquito that had recently eaten some dinosaur blood for lunch would have become trapped in the sticky substance called *resin* that oozes out of trees. Tree resin is very good at preserving whatever becomes trapped in it for a long period of time. It's a bit like nature's plastic wrap, only better.

Eventually the mosquito would become fossilized, as the resin hardened and became a substance called amber. If the scientists found the lump of amber and were able to extract dinosaur DNA from the blood inside the trapped mosquito, would they be able to use the DNA to bring dinosaurs back to life?

The main problem is that over very long periods of time the DNA does start to decay, like milk in a fridge. Bits of the DNA get lost or damaged—and you really need ALL of the information to be able to recreate a dinosaur.

Human beings share 70% of the same DNA with a slug, so you can see how important it is to have the

whole thing. You'd be disappointed if you were trying to grow a herd of veloceraptors and ended up with a matchbox full of earwigs . . .

Also, over time, the DNA of the mosquito may well have become mixed up with the dinosaur's DNA, which might produce a huge mosquitosaurus, but is more likely to result in a big pile of green goo.

But here's the worst news. Even if scientists could get a complete set of dino-DNA, they would then need to get it to assemble into chromosomes and then use the chromosomes to fertilize an egg . . . a live egg . . . a live, dinosaur egg. This is probably an impossible task and, anyway, if they had a live dinosaur egg, why would scientists bother to clone a dinosaur in the first place?

WHY AM I TIRED WHEN I HAVE JUST WOKEN UP?

It seems reasonable to expect that after being awake all day, you should feel tired. It also seems reasonable to feel more awake after you have rested. But sleepiness isn't as straightforward as that.

Your body has an "internal clock," which gives you a sense of time. For example, don't you find you often wake up just before your alarm rings in the morning? That is because of your body clock. But at certain times your internal clock doesn't work properly.

Research on very young children, babies, and toddlers shows that the longer they are awake, the sleepier they will be, just as you would expect. However, children between 10 and 12 years old are likely to be less sleepy after 10 hours of being awake than after 5 hours. They will be even less sleepy after 14 hours.

The human body releases hormones that make it sleepy when it needs rest, but at the age of about 10, and through the teenage years, the internal clock seems to delay doing this until later at night. This means teenagers often feel wide awake at about 9 P.M. or 10 P.M., just when they should be feeling sleepy. This shift of the internal clock appears to go back to normal when people get older.

It is very common for teenagers to wake up feeling tired, have a sleepy period in midafternoon, and perk up at night. As a result, some sleep experts believe that the school day—starting in the early morning and ending midafternoon—is completely wrong for kids. Teens going to bed at midnight and getting up at seven o'clock in the morning are tired and unable to concentrate. This makes their memory poor and makes them less creative. Recent research shows it would be best to allow children to start their school day later.

So what can you do if you have trouble going to sleep at bedtime? Well, experts suggest that dimming the lights at night can help your body feel sleepier, and getting lots of daylight in the morning can wake you up. Don't "binge sleep" on the weekend; get up just an hour or two later than normal. Otherwise your internal clock becomes confused. Keep your bedroom cool, dark, and quiet. Don't watch TV, surf the Internet, or listen to music right before you want to sleep. Also exercise, preferably early in the day.

Parents are often shocked when their lively kids— who used to get up at the crack of dawn full of energy—turn into lazy teenagers who can't get out of bed, yawn all day, and still want to go out at night. Now you can explain that it simply isn't your fault!

HOW LONG COULD I LIVE ON NOTHING BUT COLA?

The good news to anyone planning to live on cola alone is that it contains two of the things your body needs to survive—energy and water. This means that for the first few weeks of living on nothing but cola the worst of your problems would be sticky teeth and smelly breath.

The bad news is that cola doesn't offer much else. It doesn't contain any of the vitamins or minerals your body needs to function properly. Within a month of drinking nothing but cola, your hair would start to fall out, your nails would break easily, and your skin would become scaly and start to flake off.

The lack of a substance called *fiber,* which helps your body to poo, would mean you might spend hours sitting on the toilet clutching your stomach in agony.

Over a longer period of time the lack of essential substances called *proteins* in your diet would stop your brain from developing properly. It would stunt your growth and cause your muscles to waste away. Moreover, all the sugar in cola would also give you a large potbelly.

If you could put up with all these problems, you could probably live on nothing but cola for a long time. However, it is likely that in the end you would become depressed, go blind, pass into a coma, and die of a vitamin deficiency.

By the way, have you ever left a tooth in a glass of cola? Don't try it with your grandma's false teeth or you'll owe her a new pair, because teeth left in cola will completely disappear!
More cola, anybody?

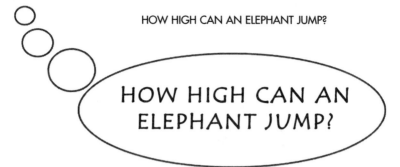

HOW HIGH CAN AN ELEPHANT JUMP?

There's an old saying:

"I bet you can't jump higher than an elephant."
"I bet I can—elephants can't jump!"

Although some people swear they have seen elephants jump, the popular point of view in scientific circles is that they can't.

One thing is certain, elephants don't really need to jump. They have no natural predators, which means that there is nothing that an elephant needs to escape from (apart from human beings who want their tusks, of course). So the ability to run and jump isn't really required.

Adult elephants are immensely strong, which means that they can usually overpower other animals without needing to run away. However, they are also massively heavy (a full-grown African elephant can weigh more than 6 tons), so scientists suspect they simply weigh too much to get airborne.

To jump, an elephant must get all four of its feet off the ground at the same time. To do this from standing still, it would have to bend and straighten its legs quickly, and propel its body upward off the ground. The muscles and bones in an elephant's legs are not designed for this. They are designed to stay very straight. Even when walking, an elephant sways from side to side, to minimize the amount of bend required in each of its legs.

How about elephants managing a running jump? A study by Stanford University in California revealed that elephants do seem to run—something that had previously been thought unlikely. The study showed that when elephants are moving quickly (they can reach speeds of more than 16 miles [25 km] per hour), their weight bounces up and down. The scientists thought this "bouncing" was more like running than walking. However, they believed that the elephants always kept one of their four feet in contact with the ground.

What if the answer to the question is that elephants jump only when no one is looking?

HOW DOES MEDICINE MAKE ME FEEL BETTER?

Your body is a staggeringly complicated biological machine—so complicated that some of the amazing things it does are still not fully understood by scientists.

Your body acts as a little factory—taking stuff like food, water, and oxygen in and using it to produce the chemicals it needs to work properly. Different organs in your body make different chemicals for different reasons.

When a disease makes one of these functions fail, you may fall ill. Then, your body might produce too much of one chemical, or not enough, or it might send the chemical to the wrong part of your body. For example, some people suffer from an illness called *diabetes*. This is caused when their bodies have problems making a chemical called *insulin*, which helps to regulate the amount of glucose in their blood. A lack of insulin can make people experience a variety of symptoms, including feeling very tired and thirsty.

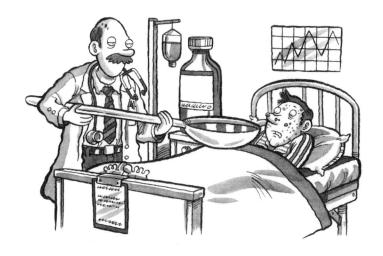

As scientists continue to find out what each of the body's organs do, which chemicals the organs make, and where those chemicals need to go, they have also been able to figure out how to copy the chemicals in laboratories.

A chemical your body requires can be injected straight into your body, or comes in the form of a pill, which you swallow. The pill is digested in your stomach, and the chemical (or medicine) gets released into your blood by your liver. Then it travels around the body until it reaches the part of your body that needs it. Once there it will do its job, just as if your body had produced the chemical itself. Ideally, that solves the problem and makes you feel better.

Alternatively, if your body is producing too much of one chemical, a medicine can be used to reduce the amount your body is creating.

Medicine rarely "cures" an illness. It just replaces or changes a function that your body normally performs on its own. If your body starts working properly again, the doctor may say you can stop taking the medicine. If it doesn't, you have to keep taking the medicine so that your body can stay healthy.

IS THERE LIFE ON OTHER PLANETS?

There is, as yet, no proof that life exists on other planets. No one knows if there are intelligent beings elsewhere in the universe. Scientists don't even know if there are really simple forms of life, like bugs or bacteria, elsewhere in the universe.

Over the years, people have claimed they have seen aliens and flying saucers. Some even say that they have been taken on board alien spaceships, or to

distant planets. Scientists, however, have never been able to find any evidence to back up these claims.

The collection of chemicals that make up the Earth, together with its size, density, distance from the sun, its atmosphere, climate, and some other factors, all work together to make the Earth a perfect place for lots of different life forms to exist. It seems unlikely that there is another planet that has all the right ingredients to support life, spinning around another star.

Scientists studying the most likely places that life might be found near Earth—the planet Mars and some of the moons around Jupiter and Saturn—haven't given up looking, but the signs aren't very promising. For 40 years they have been sending radio signals out into deep space, but as yet, no one has answered.

None of this means that there is no life out there. The universe contains billions and billions of stars. Several billion of these could have a system of planets around them, like our solar system. Some astronomers believe that the sheer size of the universe means that it is likely that there are planets where life has developed in some form.

The search continues. In the future, new telescopes should be able to detect the presence of chemicals around planets orbiting nearby stars. They will search the nearest star system to ours, which is called Alpha Centauri. Though it is the nearest star system, Alpha Centauri isn't really very near, being about 25 trillion miles (41 trillion km) away.

The radio signals scientists send out in the hope that an intelligent life-form might respond could be replaced with laser-based communications. These signals could be accurately fired out deep into space.

As for the likelihood of aliens visiting our planet, scientists think the distances are just too huge. Any spaceships coming here would have to travel for years to get here. Even if they came from the nearest star system, Alpha Centauri, and the craft could travel at the speed of light, it would take them 4.3 years to get here. Human technology is a long way away from developing a craft that can travel that fast, and currently scientists believe that nothing can travel faster than light.

So unless aliens have technology a lot more advanced than human beings, and can travel in ways human beings haven't discovered yet, the chance of meeting an extraterrestrial being any time soon is very slim.

DO MEN OR WOMEN DRIVE BETTER?

Next time you hear your mom and dad arguing about who is the better driver, know the facts.

Studies have shown that young men, aged 25 and below, have more accidents than women of the same age. Young males tend to drive faster and take more risks, and consequently crash more often than any other group of drivers.

Studies also show that women over the age of 25 are more likely to have minor accidents, such as bumping into stationary vehicles while parking. Men over 25 have fewer accidents, but theirs tend to be more serious. They are also more likely to hit objects, such as walls and pedestrians.

Experts agree these statistics are partly because of the fact that women do more shopping and therefore spend more time in parking lots. Men tend to do more highway driving at higher speeds.

Another factor that could explain this is that there are differences between a man's brain and a woman's brain. Some of these differences are caused by chemicals in our bodies, mostly by a group of female hormones called *estrogens* and a male hormone called *testosterone*. These hormones affect a baby's brain and its behavior after birth.

Studies indicate that estrogens help the brain develop the ability to switch attention from one thing to another quickly. In theory, this would make women better able to deal with sudden changes in road conditions, such as unexpected traffic, and this could make women less likely to have accidents.

Testosterone, on the other hand, has been shown to increase a brain's ability to judge spaces. This is useful when estimating distances and the size of things, and in theory, this could make men better at doing things such as parking a car and reading a map.

Remember, this is very sensitive information. Reveal it during a car trip and you may be involved in an accident yourself!

WHAT'S THE WORST-SMELLING THING IN THE WORLD?

You will probably have your own opinion on what smells horrendous—you might even say your brother's bedroom. It's very much a matter of personal taste, but most people will agree that any list of the most vile-smelling things would include dog poo, vomit, farts, smelly feet, bad breath, and rotting eggs or meat.

When choosing the worst-smelling thing in the world, you need to choose something that not only smells bad, but smells very strongly. For this it is necessary to examine the chemistry of stinkiness. Certain chemicals and chemical compounds pop up again and again in bad-smell situations. These include hydrogen sulfide (which makes rotten eggs smell gross) and butryric acid (which lends its distinctive bouquet to some of the riper scented cheeses, sweaty feet, and rancid butter).

All of the above smell worse in a laboratory than they do in nature. The merest whiff of a concentrated dose of any of them would have you bringing up your lunch in the blink of a teary eye.

Cadaverine and putrescine are responsible for the smell of dead flesh, and methanethiol is produced by decomposing vegetable matter and adds a cabbagey whiff to farts and bad breath. Aroid titanum, also known as the giant corpse flower, is generally agreed to have a smell not unlike a rotting corpse. For this reason it is probably best avoided as a Mother's Day gift.

But the mother and father of all serious stinks is butyl seleno mercaptan. This is the stuff that gives the spray produced by a skunk its terrible smell, a smell that clings to things. It's so bad that people who have been hit by the spray often end up burning their clothes to get rid of the stink.

Butyl seleno, and its close relatives ethyl and methyl mercaptan, are so awful that governments have investigated their potential uses for controlling rioting crowds and making military-grade stink bombs. The stench is so powerful that it can be detected even when diluted to two parts in a million. For this reason, tiny amounts are added to odorless natural gas so that leaks can be detected. It is said to smell like a powerful combination of rotting cabbage, garlic, onions, burned toast, and sewer gas.

IF I COULD EAT ONLY ONE FOOD FOREVER, WHICH SHOULD I CHOOSE?

The human body requires a complex range of proteins, vitamins, minerals, and fats to survive. For this reason nutritionists recommend you eat a varied diet to make sure you get everything you need. There is probably no single thing you can eat that gives you everything your body needs, but what comes closest?

Some fruits, especially prunes, blueberries, and pomegranates, have been found to be particularly good for humans. They contain loads of vitamins and fiber, but also antioxidants. These are chemicals that protect cells in the body from damage.

Acai, a berry found on palm trees in Brazil and the Amazon jungle, may be the world's most nutritious fruit. Containing an impressive collection of healthy vitamins and minerals, protein and fiber, it is also a rich source of amino and fatty acids. These help to slow down the body's aging process, and might even be a treatment for some cancers. Better still, the berries taste like cherries and chocolate, too!

113

If you like slimy vegetation, seaweed may be an even
better choice than acai berries. It is rich in vitamins
and minerals, but also contains more protein than
meat, and more calcium than milk. Seaweed also
helps the body to heal, and will keep your hair and
skin healthy. It will help to prevent high blood
pressure and will boost your body's resistance to
disease and infection. Seaweed has even been found
to protect against the effects of pollution and
radiation poisoning. In Japan, people consume a lot
of seaweed, and the Japanese live longer and fewer
of them suffer from heart disease than almost
anywhere else in the world.

The problem with seaweed is that it contains very few calories, so you'd have to eat a lot of it to get the energy your body needs.

Starchy root vegetables, such as the sweet potato, the Peruvian maca, or Oriental kudzu, are good all-around foods. Kudzu, for example, has more calories per gram than honey, but the energy you get from it will last a lot longer. It also contains a range of useful vitamins and minerals, and is used to relieve a number of ailments from headaches to chicken pox.

It is possible that you could live quite well on any of these foods, as all of them contain most of the important ingredients you need to live. In time, however, the things they lack—a vitamin missing here, a protein there—would probably have some negative effects on your body. There really is no food in nature that does it all . . .

. . . or is there?

Bee pollen might be the closest thing in nature to a perfect food. Pollen is the fine powder that flowers produce to fertilize seeds to make new flowers. Bees collect it from flowers. They mix it with their spit and nectar (a sweet liquid also produced by flowers) to make honey. Scientists have studied the possibility of using pollen as a medicine and a food supplement. Athletes use it to boost energy and help them perform better. Records dating back five thousand years praise its nutritious and healing qualities. Some experts believe that it contains all the necessary nutrients for human survival.

Some nutritionists have stated that in theory, you could live a healthy life on just bee pollen and water. The only downsides would appear to be a possible allergic reaction (pollen is the stuff that causes hay fever), the difficulty of collecting it (currently achieved by a wire grid with a dish underneath at the door of the beehive), and the fact that the coating around each pollen grain is so tough it can preserve the contents for a million years. This makes the process of preparing it for eating very expensive.

WHICH ANIMAL IS THE DEADLIEST IN THE WORLD?

Mosquitoes kill more people every year than any other animal, through spreading malaria and other fatal diseases. Estimates put the annual death toll from mosquito-carried malaria alone at more than two and a half million. This is far higher than the number of people killed by any other animal. Even human beings with all that military hardware at their disposal don't kill that many people a year.

It's hard to measure one animal against another when it comes to deadliness. Environment is an important factor—the outcome of a fight between

117

a great white shark and a Bengal tiger would depend quite a lot on whether it took place in the Pacific Ocean or the forests of East India.

Sharks and tigers are certainly dangerous, but not all deadly creatures have huge slavering jaws full of razor-sharp teeth. A poisonous or venomous creature can kill things many times its own size. More than fifty thousand people are killed each year by poisonous snakes alone, with the Asian cobra topping the table for numbers.

The prize for the creature with the strongest poison probably goes to the golden dart frog. For thousands of years, tribesmen in the South American rain forest where the frogs live have used the poison that covers this frog's skin to tip arrows for hunting and warfare. Just two micrograms of this poison can kill a person. To give you an idea how much that is, there are about six micrograms of ink contained in the period at the end of this sentence.

Another contender for World's Most Lethal Creature is the Australian box jellyfish. Its body is only about the size of a salad bowl, but its tentacles (and there are up to 60 of them) can be 15-feet (4.5-m) long with up to five thousand stinging cells on each. Just one box jellyfish contains enough venom to kill 60 adult humans. Is this why so many Australians are really good at swimming?

WHAT MAKES SOMETHING FUNNY?

Different people laugh at different things, and cultural differences often mean that the sense of humor can be entirely different from one country to the next—so a joke that is hilarious in one place might fall flat in another. According to a recent scientific study of jokes, British, Irish, Australian, and New Zealand audiences like jokes involving wordplays and puns, whereas Americans and Canadians prefer jokes where someone is made to look stupid. Germans laugh at more jokes than anyone else, and Japanese people hardly ever tell jokes at all.

But though humor doesn't always translate, most people seem to laugh at three things in particular. First when they feel superior and are pleased with themselves, second when they feel relief and stress or tension disappears, and thirdly when they are surprised by something that doesn't make sense.

If someone falls over but is not hurt—by slipping on a banana peel, for example—you might feel relief that they are OK, and also superiority because they look stupid and you didn't fall over.

Part of the scientific study was to try to find the world's funniest joke. Thousands were submitted and people all around the world voted for their favorites. It was won by this entry:

A couple of hunters are out in the woods when one of them falls to the ground. He doesn't seem to be breathing, and his eyes are rolled back in his head. The other hunter whips out his cell phone and calls the emergency services.

"My friend is dead! What can I do?" he gasps to the operator.

"Just take it easy. I can help. First, let's make sure he's dead," says the operator, in a calm, soothing voice.

There is silence; then a shot is heard.

The guy's voice comes back on the line. He says, "OK, now what?"

Scientists conducting the study concluded that the punch line to this joke had all three elements— the superiority over the dumb hunter, the relief of tension, and the element of surprise.

It may not be the funniest joke you ever heard, but more people around the world found it funny than any other joke submitted to the study, so the title is deserved!

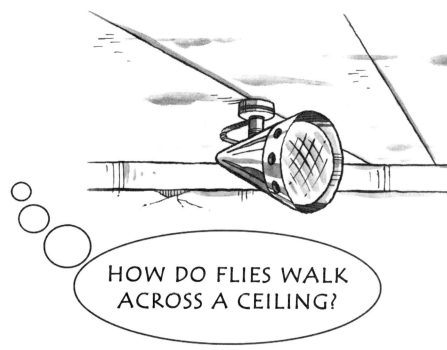

HOW DO FLIES WALK ACROSS A CEILING?

The first thing to take into account when answering this question is that flies don't weigh very much. Therefore the pull of gravity on a fly isn't as strong as it is on a person. Still, the fly possesses an impressive range of special equipment that enables it to remain attached to the ceiling while upside down.

Flies' feet each have two pads covered in tiny hairs called *setae*. The setae are curved and rounded at the ends and act a bit like suction cups, helping the fly cling on to the ceiling.

The feet produce a mixture of sugars and oils, which results in just enough foot stickiness to keep the fly in place while still allowing it to walk about.

Each foot also has a pair of tiny claws. These allow the fly to grip microscopic cracks in the ceiling. To make sure the fly doesn't get stuck permanently to a surface, the claws enable it to twist and peel its feet off the ceiling.

A fly usually keeps four of its six feet in contact with a ceiling at all times. That way, it can't walk very fast, but at least two-thirds of it is attached at all times, making it less likely to fall.

Flies can walk a lot quicker when they are the right way up, but to get from one place to another it is quicker for a fly to ... well, fly.

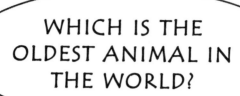

WHICH IS THE OLDEST ANIMAL IN THE WORLD?

The main difficulty when answering this question is that it is very hard for scientists to prove an animal's age accurately. It really helps if an animal has been under observation its whole life.

The oldest chimpanzee in the world, for example, is said to be one called Cheeta, who appeared in Tarzan movies in the 1930s. Cheeta recently celebrated his 75th birthday. There might well be older chimps in the jungles of Borneo, but no one knows for sure.

The oldest bird in the world might well be a parrot that belonged to Winston Churchill (Great Britain's prime minister during the Second World War). Charlie, a blue macaw, is thought by his owner to be 104 years old. After 1964, Charlie lived in a pet shop, but he was banned for upsetting the customers by swearing. It seems Churchill had taught Charlie to shout rude things about Adolf Hitler.

Giant Galapagos tortoises are famous for living long lives. There is one, named Harriet, who lived in

a zoo in Queensland, Australia. She died in 2006, at the ripe old age of 176. Just a few months earlier, Adwaita, an Aldabra giant tortoise, died in Alipore Zoo in India, at an estimated (but unproven) age of 250 years.

The ocean is a good place to live if you want to live a long time. Geoducks (a type of clam) regularly live to about 146. The oldest ever found was 160. Counting the rings on a geoduck's shell is a very reliable way of figuring out how old it is. To make it to a ripe old age, however, these creatures have to avoid being eaten by humans, cooked with pasta and a nice cream sauce.

Bowheads are a type of whale that have been hunted in the waters around the coast of Alaska for centuries. In 2007, a bowhead whale was found that had a fragment of a weapon embedded in its blubber. The fragment was probably the result of a failed hunting expedition. Experts can date it, quite accurately, back to the 1890s, and this would make the whale between 115 and 130 years old.

The grandaddy of the oceans, however, is generally agreed to be the deep sea tube worm, *lamellibrachia luymesi*. Lurking at the bottom of the ocean, the worms look a bit like giant lipsticks. Marine scientists can assess the age of the worms from their size and the speed at which they grow. Studies have shown they can live for up to 250 years, which makes it a good bet for world's oldest animal.